The Playbook

A Student-Athlete's Guide to Success

ROBERT GRILLI

ISBN-13: 978-1533573810
ISBN-10: 1533573816

Cover by Melody Johnson

Table of Contents

Dedication

To Mom, Dad, and Thomas:

From driving through snow storms to get me to practice to surprising me and seeing my first collegiate hit. For pushing me to do my best in academics and athletics, and for having my back through the failures and successes. For without you three nothing would be possible. Thank you and love you.

To My Readers:

A playbook prepares you to succeed on the field. This playbook attempts to serve a similar function both on and off the field and offer tips and tools that draw on experiences of a former student-athlete's personal growth over two decades. I trust my journey and the tools I have utilized to succeed academically, athletically and socially will empower current and prospective student-athletes alike. It will also empower family, friends, coaches, and faculty to connect and help their student-athletes thrive. I wish you the best as you embark on this exciting chapter of your life.

Acknowledgements

This book would not be possible without the contributions of the following people and organizations to my academic, athletic, and personal growth:

St. Michael's College: Thank you for instilling in me *"Goodness, Discipline, and Knowledge"* (Psalm 118). Thank you, Mr. Corrrente, Mr. Lumsden and Coach Zownir.

Salt Lake Community College Baseball Staff: Derek "Wadd" Waddoups and DG Nelson: You believed in me when no other college coaches in the nation did. Thank you for giving me my first opportunity to play collegiately and for helping me develop into an adult on and off the field.

To My Teammates and Friends: Living away from home hasn't always been easy. Thank you for what I know will be life-long friendships, for always welcoming me into your homes over the holidays and for making my college experience great. In particular, Thank You: Patrick Weigel, Brady Corless, Paul and Cal Quantrill, Maxx and Molly Tissenbaum, Blake Fox, Connor Hollis, Jordan Stading, Michael Pyeatt, Ryan Grippo, Blair Hamilton, Matt Scobie, Duane Notice, David Longville, TJ Baker, Julia Orsini, Jessica & Nicholas Ursitti, Steven Adam and Georgi Dolence.

Dr. Richard Scamell: On behalf of all the student-athletes at The University of Houston, thank you for your support as our NCAA Faculty Athletics Representative. Personally, thank you for your guidance, mentoring and honest feedback.

Dr. Emese Felvégi: Your selflessness, passion and willingness to help no matter the task is greatly appreciated and for that I Thank You.

Coach Lee Fiocchi: Thank You for your approachability, words of wisdom, honesty, and for helping me find clarity and pushing me to be an empowered leader in every facet of my life.

Thank you, University of Houston Support Staff. The sense of community, support and open lines of communication truly allowed each and every student-athlete I know including myself to thrive and achieve great success. Thank you Lauren Dubois, Lori Selzer, Sasha Blake, Sarah Maples, Traci Cauley, Maria Peden, DeJuena Chizer, Hunter Yurachek, and the baseball coaching staff.

Foreword

I am a fan of Dave Isay, the founder of StoryCorps and author of books such as *Listening Is An Act of Love* and *Callings: The Purpose and Passion of Work*. In a fashion somewhat similar to that in these books, with the reader acting as a facilitator, *The Playbook: A Student-Athlete's Guide to Success* is in essence a conversation between the author, Robert Grilli, and young people (the facilitators) who aspire to be successful student-athletes. Along the way in the book Robert shares personal stories and important lessons he has learned about characteristics it takes to be successful both as a student and an athlete – characteristics such as industriousness, enthusiasm, friendship, loyalty, cooperation, self-control, intellectual curiosity, initiative, persistence, adaptability, and resourcefulness. A member of the University of Houston baseball team for two years, this book puts words to Robert's actions as a University of Houston Cougar. The sincerity and pride contained in what he has to say reflect his strong desire to be an encouragement to those whose lives he touches.

Richard Scamell, Professor
Department of Decision and Information Sciences
Associate Dean for Student Affairs
C. T. Bauer College of Business
University of Houston
NCAA Faculty Athletics Representative

Pre-Game

Setting The Table

"Someone once told me not to bite off more than I can chew. I said I'd rather choke on greatness than nibble on mediocrity." -Unknown

In my Junior year at the University of Houston, one of my professors asked me to record a video for the class explaining what allowed me to have success in the course while training and playing baseball, which consumed twenty hours of my week. After sharing tips with my peers through this video, I started to write notes in my cellphone about my experiences and the various tools I developed that would help my younger brother as he entered college. I then realized that he would not be the only one who could benefit from the knowledge I have accumulated spanning two decades playing baseball and growing as an individual. Throughout this book I will put forth various strategies and tips that will allow you to be empowered to succeed in a variety of situations and scenarios that are inherent to the demanding life of a student-athlete.

I harken back to a key event that occurred during my elementary school days, which had a major impact on my life and has continuously spurred me on to **prove the naysayers wrong**. During my formative years I had always wanted to attend a prestigious prep school named St. Michael's College School (SMC, in downtown Toronto, Canada) and had always set goals to achieve this. One day I shared this aspiration with my Grade 8 teacher who was quick to reply in a sarcastic tone saying, "Good luck with that." What this teacher was echoing was a familiar refrain among all my teachers at that time, who said "Robert has so much potential but he's just not showing it and it is reflected in the subpar quality of his work." I took this as a slight, and have used it to my advantage since then. I have developed an attitude of constantly attempting to **Prove em Wrong** in both sport and school.

It's worth noting that there were other reasons for attending SMC including its sense of community, the benefits associated with an actively engaged alumni network, and its excellent reputation in academics and sports. The path that I took upon attending SMC mirrored the college recruiting process in selecting a school and ensuring a proper fit for me.

1st Inning

Process Over Outcome

"The prize is in the process." -Baron Baptiste

People often talk about a "defining moment" as if it was a sole event that leads to a certain outcome. I would like to challenge the idea of "defining moments" based on the principle of *process over outcome.* Sure, there are outliers where a certain event can abruptly change your life forever, but when we look at things day by day, every moment, every word, every action, and every decision is, in and of itself, a defining moment. Collectively these defining moments constitute the "process" that shapes you into being you.

When you win a championship, whether it is a state championship, a bowl game, a volleyball championship, college cup, or a college world series, you may remember hoisting the trophy but in time, you will come to realize that its the process that got you there that's special. Oftentimes people get too caught up in the result, and forget to take the necessary steps that will allow for them to achieve the result. They make these moments out to be this big make or break thing. They are just adding unnecessary pressure. Concentrating on the process rather than the outcome allows you to continue to prepare and dominate each task while the end goal takes care of itself.

Throughout this book I will take you through the process outlining each step, task, and lesson I've learned that have made me successful. This will include preparedness, interpersonal skills, engagement on the field and in the classroom, seeking assistance when needed, "compete mode", and the Golden Tools. These steps and more will empower and allow for you to succeed and dominate situations and scenarios that are part of the daily life of a student-athlete.

2nd Inning

A Goal Setting Exercise

"I think goals should never be easy, they should force you to work, even if they are uncomfortable at the time." -Michael Phelps

Prior to continuing reading this book I would like you to take a few minutes to set your goals for the year using the space below. This is an exercise that I completed before each school year. Be sure to include academic, athletic, and social goals. Under each goal, write down one or two steps that will be instrumental in achieving the goal. There is something that happens when one writes down their goals that can't really be explained, other than when they are written down they become tangible and real, and you are more likely to commit yourself to achieving those goals. When you look back at the end of the year you will be amazed how many goals you will have achieved.

ACADEMIC GOALS

(e.g., Achieve 4.0 GPA, Academic All Region, Dean's list, Graduate)

ATHLETIC GOALS

____
____
____
____
____
____
____
____
____
____
____
____

(e.g., Earn a starting position, Win a Conference/National Championship, various others)

SOCIAL GOALS

____
____
____
____
____
____
____
____
____
____

(e.g., Surround yourself with great friends who support you through the good and bad).

3rd Inning

The Transition

"At some point in our lives our athletic ability will fade away, but what no one can take away from us is our mind." -Robert Grilli

What makes the best collegiate athletes so great, and what makes them so successful is their ability to live in the moment. A college quarterback who is in the so called "red zone" with less than a minute to go, has just missed converting on third down but is now focused on going for it on fourth down with blatant disregard for the failure that has just occurred. **The best competitors and most successful athletes are those who live in the moment.** If he thinks "Dang I need to make this completion or our season is over" then he starts a negative thought process, which will take him out of the moment, and will undoubtedly make him less successful. If he executes the play call, thereby focusing on the PROCESS, then the outcome will take care of itself.

What I am challenging you to do here is to take a step back, think about your future, and where you will be in 5, 10, 15, or 20 years because at some point in your life your athletic ability will no longer be there, whether that be at 18, 21, or 36 years of age. Each person's window of athletic opportunity is different, and I challenge you to think about what you have to "fall back on" when your window closes. This is a harsh reality and going through this myself, these words didn't ring true until I was in my last year of eligibility. In my case I was left wondering whether or not the Major League Baseball draft would work out, so I began thinking that I had to begin searching for alternate prospects (i.e., certain jobs or industries that either suited or interested me). Once this began to sink in, going to school didn't seem so much like the hand me down clothes anymore in comparison to getting a job which always seemed to me as the brand new Jordan's.

In school I essentially juggled on average 5 different jobs. My 5 jobs included 5 different courses per semester, 6 including baseball. The more I thought about it, the more it started to sink in that in the real world I would not have the same variety of tasks on a daily basis, and perhaps it would be more of a mundane existence, which was difficult to wrap my head around. There are so many people and athletic departments that put an emphasis on the transition from collegiate sports to life after sport and this reality was starting to really hit me. However, what allayed these concerns for me was that I had a backup plan in place, which gave me a certain peace of mind.

What I'm referring to is a college degree and the intangibles that a student-athlete inherently develops in going through this collegiate path. **This includes the ability to work as part of a team to achieve a common goal, and the ability to work in high-pressure situations.** By comparison, the aforementioned qualities will allow a student-athlete to perform in ways that many of one's peers are not as proficient at in a professional setting.

I will outline a number of tools and skills associated with being a high level athlete, provide you with a variety of life lessons that will erase many of the unknowns that exist in a classroom environment. This will also enable you to have a "fall back plan" as you transition from student-athlete to a productive and successful member of the working world.

4th Inning

An Athlete's Preparedness

"Success is where preparation and opportunity meet."
-Bobby Unser

As an athlete, one of the best tools that contribute to your success in your respective sport is your preparation. This preparation encompasses what you do in the weight room, the training/technique developed in practice and game-plans/scouting reports going into big games. **When you have worked this PROCESS, the big game doesn't seem so daunting and you are not met with nervousness stemming from anxiety.** Instead, you experience healthy anxiousness or excitement as a result of anticipation and a desire to dominate whatever it is that stands in front of you. This same level of preparation is what will allow you to have success in the classroom.

The first step that will help you start off "on the right foot" to succeed academically is to implement the use of an agenda/calendar in your everyday life. I have always used a printed version, one that I carry around in my backpack and pull out when needed. I make entries with pen or pencil as I can color code it and have the freedom to write anywhere on the page. I always preferred to purchase calendars sold at our school's bookstore as the dates of key school events were included and therefore directly related to my everyday school life. Also, some athletic departments provide student-athletes with agendas that have the athletic schedules of each team already in place. Some may prefer an electronic calendar and that is okay as long as you make sure to "plan the work and work the plan." Technology is constantly changing: when I shared this tip with classmates/teammates, they began to use the agenda/calendar on their cellphones. The benefit of using an electronic calendar is that you can set up a number of alerts and it's also more easily accessible. Many websites have the capability to **sync your athletic calendar directly from the website to your computer, phone, or tablet.** This is another way to help you stay organized and keep you on track.

It may take some trial and error, but once you have selected which method you are going to use, it is crucial at the beginning of each semester to take time to review every syllabus and write down all the due dates of each quiz, assignment and exam that you'll have for the semester along with your team's schedule. The use of an agenda is especially important for online classes, as these due dates and assignments are a lot easier to miss than classes with face-to-face lectures. Obviously these dates are subject to change, but with your daily use of this tool I assure you that you will rarely (if ever) miss or be unprepared for an assignment, quiz or exam. Immediately upon returning to your residence after your school/athletic day is complete, be sure to look over what you need to complete for that evening and in the coming days.

On Fridays it's good to know what you have to complete for the weekend but, at the same time, it's important to take a longer range look at the following week's schedule to ensure that you are prepared for whatever lies ahead. The agenda is similar to the weight room, as some may like it while others may not. However, regardless of this fact you will begin to understand its value and will see the payoff when it comes time to compete in the classroom.

16 MONDAY *POLS EXAM*
137/229
GENB: Check if project Available
MARK: See if extra credit open
* ECON: * FINISH Edits for ECON project *
- Call Dad
- Make Spring sched
- Math tutor: 12:30-1:30

17 TUESDAY *ECON memo 3 Due *
138/228
Math: Homework & Quiz
- Study for exam
POLS: Quiz
ACCT: LS
- Brief GENB Proff about missing class Next week

18 WEDNESDAY
139/227
ACCT: Get ahead b/c of game tomorrow
ACCT Tutor: 5-6pm

5th Inning

Interpersonal Skills and Class Participation

"Wise men speak because they have something to say; Fools because they have to say something." -Plato

As a former student-athlete, I understand the time constraints that are placed upon the student-athlete, and that's why I have written a relatively short book (70 pages total, and if you plan ahead to read 10 pages a night and you'll be done in 7 days) outlining specific tools in a manner that will directly benefit your daily life. Everyone's learning style is different; some students are visual learners while others are auditory learners or musical learners. Some are more hands on while others enjoy reading textbooks. I am amazed by how some people are able to memorize the lyrics of songs. If this is something that works for you, tap into your strong memorization skills.

Throughout my four-year college career I did not solely rely on reading the textbook for the course but also went to class to listen to the professor. After creating a detailed calendar, the next step in the PROCESS of achieving success as a student-athlete is **going to class**. Getting up early to go to class after a killer practice and workout might not seem necessary in the moment, but it is a decision that is crucial to the process for a number of reasons. First of all, professors may have "mandatory attendance" that could be worth anywhere from 5% to 10% of your overall grade in the course. That's up to 10% in addition to whatever grades you earn on your assignments and exams. That's HUGE!

This attendance check can be done through a physical roll call or through "clicker questions." This can be either a binary result (0 or 1) based on whether or not you attended the class or they may base attendance points on accuracy or a combination of both. It's good to keep in mind that clicker questions are very relevant, and it is a good idea to write the question and answer down, as you will most likely see this question again on an exam.

Another reason why it is so important to attend class is so that you can take notes: this helped me evolve from a good student to a great student. Personally, I tried to sit in the front two rows: because (a) there are fewer distractions, (b) your face becomes familiar to your professor and they will recognize you. This makes it easier for you to approach them given your level of familiarity and continuous, active attendance.

I believe that reading just the textbook is like giving someone a generic workout plan: you'll see some gains but if you had a "sport specific" plan your gains would be far greater. Now don't get me wrong, sometimes textbooks are absolutely required, as professors will tell you whether or not the course requires the textbook or not. Furthermore, the material on their PowerPoint slides or during their lectures will most likely be derived from that very same textbook. They may ask you to pull information from the textbooks that you'll have to go back and analyze, and possibly cite the material afterwards. While taking Accounting during the last semester of my senior year, it wasn't until I started reading the textbook that I was able to be successful in the course, despite attending every lecture and taking detailed notes. However, textbooks can be quite expensive and it doesn't make sense to purchase a textbook if the course doesn't require it or your scholarship doesn't cover the cost of books. Look for e-book versions of your textbooks if that is how you like to read. They may be a bit cheaper, too.

Your class notes are your preparation and represent your "academic specific" workout plan. They allow you to digest the information that you were taught in a way that helps you understand the material covered in class. Professors tend to give hints during lectures that will help you with assignments and information as to what will be on exams. Every time a professor gave a hint about material that would show up on an exam I would put a star and a box around it so when I went to study for the exam I could place an emphasis on knowing that material.

By going to class you show the professor that you genuinely care about the course, the material, and what they have to say. What you need to understand is that professors don't teach because they didn't have any other options and thought to themselves "heck I guess I'll just get my PhD and teach at a university." No, they have a burning passion for what they do, what they research, and what they teach their students. Their lectures are their games: don't be disruptive. Being on your cell phone during class would be the equivalent to someone booing you at a home game. Not to mention it takes away from your learning experience, as you won't be able to grasp all of the information being taught. Sitting in the front two rows will make it difficult for you to get away with having your cellphone out, regardless of the cell phone policy that the professor has set out.

Another important aspect of going to class is connecting with other students. It is necessary to have a support group, a brotherhood or sisterhood relationship with your team and teammates, but it is also necessary to make contacts with members of your classes who are not student-athletes. As a student-athlete you will inevitably miss class, and there are certain things said during class that are not covered in textbooks or on PowerPoint slides (as those are just the blueprints in terms of the material covered during class). It is imperative you make contacts/friends who aren't student-athletes because they will be on a different schedule and you will be able to fill in each other on what you missed. By sitting in the front two rows, you are surrounded by individuals who share the same desire to succeed, and they will be able to give you reliable information. This leads me into my next point: developing relationships with your professors is a beneficial by-product of going to class regularly.

6th Inning

Engaging Your Professors and Teaching Assistants

"The dream begins with a teacher who believes in you, who tugs and pushes and leads you to the next plateau, sometimes poking you with a sharp stick called 'truth'." -Dan Rather

At the beginning of each semester, usually within the first week, I would go up to my professors, introduce myself and say something like "Hi Dr.___. My name is Robert Grilli and I am on the baseball team here at the University of Houston. I'm looking forward to your course and if anything comes up from a baseball scheduling standpoint that conflicts with your course I will let you know well in advance and I will ensure that my course obligations are looked after." I did this regardless of whether the class was 25, 100, 300, or 700 students. .

This helped to fight the myth that I had heard throughout my high school days that "once you go to a university you are just a number, they don't care about you." This could not be more erroneous; you are only a number if YOU make yourself a number.

Most professors appreciate when you take the time to engage them, but keep in mind that some of them may have a one-dimensional view of student-athletes. On occasion, professors may state that they will not allow you to miss any classes, excused absences or not, and as a consequence, will not work with you or your athletic schedule. As a result, you may need to find another course or if it is a required course for your major, you will need to work through it and try to win over the professor, sometimes getting help from an academic advisor or other staff member. Unfortunately, this does happen but if you do your homework on professors by using various websites that provide feedback about them as well as asking upperclassmen about their experiences with certain professors, (older student-athletes) the chances of you running into this problem will diminish significantly.

There are many stereotypes that we face every day. I even had a professor who held the fact that I was from Canada against me, however, the biggest stereotype that student-athletes face is that of being just a "jock." The "jock" only cares about his sport, and is not interested in taking advantage of the academic opportunities he has as a student-athlete. I made it my mission throughout my collegiate academic career to change this perception with every one of my professors. Stereotypes may also be based on what sport you play, so you may have to work harder to build these relationships with your professors and rid yourself of these preconceived labels, regardless of whether they are justified or not. A Student-Athlete Climate study at Pennsylvania State University found that "interactions with faculty will yield the largest "pay-off" for student-athletes (Rankin, et. al, 2011, p. 8), so be mindful of this and build rapport.

By sitting in the front row and identifying yourself as a student-athlete, you make yourself accountable to the professor, and they will notice if you do not show up to class. This identification process helps when you email a professor to schedule times to meet with them during their office hours for assistance, or to make up missed lectures due to travel or competition. Furthermore, if you are struggling, but exhibit a consistent concerted effort most professors will do everything they can to help you succeed in their course. To prove that you are a responsible student, be sure to show up for class consistently, on time, all the while working towards developing a rapport with your respective professors. These relationships may not end after you complete the course, as many of your professors may serve as valuable contacts for you in the future. **In today's society, networking is extremely important whether one is trying to find a job or garnering information to assist you in a myriad of ways.**

In fact, upon completion of each of my courses I would ask my professor if they would be one of my references. Following the guidelines that I have put forth in this book is a major reason why my professors have never refused to serve as one of my references. Many career services personnel within the athletic department and school strongly urge student-athletes to set up a LinkedIn account in order to start building an extensive professional network. After completing each of my courses I would ask the respective professor if they would connect with me on LinkedIn.

I would like to share a personal example of building relationships with professors. While enrolled in a business class I developed an excellent relationship with a professor, who was a very successful businessman for a large financial services firm. At the completion of the course the professor introduced me to one of his partners who had taken a similar path with respect to sports and education, which led him to become a very successful businessman. Through this connection I received valuable insight, guidance, and mentoring while building two great networking contacts. Had I not introduced myself, put myself under a microscope, and performed under a spotlight, I would have missed this opportunity to develop a value added relationship.

7th Inning

Overtime

"Effort is important but knowing where to make an effort makes all the difference." –Unknown

Once you have reached the point where you are attending classes regularly and taking good class notes, there is one more piece of the puzzle that encourages academic success. Homework completion typically makes up a percentage of your grade, and this is something not just to be viewed as a requirement but as an opportunity as well. I say this because the better your score is for homework assignments, the more it will provide a cushion when it comes exam time. When you have a high homework grade and excellent class attendance, this "mark cushion" is further increased when teachers offer extra credit. **There is no substitute for hard work, and you must work diligently to complete all tasks.**

However, there are always ways to work smarter as well. One way to work smarter is to understand the grading scale and use it to your advantage. When you look to enroll in a course, seek out a course syllabus from the previous year, for that particular professor and note the grading breakdown and then decide whether or not this breakdown makes it possible to build a "marks cushion."

Some Athletic Departments provide tutors who are able to help one understand course material as well as break down key concepts. There were times in class when topics were covered too quickly or I was required to miss a day of class due to a baseball commitment. If I still didn't understand the material after receiving the material from a classmate, I would then go to a tutor to clarify those concepts.

Student-athletes are proud individuals and are sometimes not willing to ask for help. There are student-athletes who may think that they do not need tutors and that's okay. However, there is no shame in asking for help if you need it. Also, one of the benefits of using a tutor within your athletic department is that it does not cost anything extra to you as it is covered by the department.

Working in groups can assist you as well, but you must be sure that it is permissible in the particular course, as some professors will allow group work while others may not. Some courses will offer learning labs on campus with a free tutoring service that go along with the course. For instance, at the University of Houston, my Management Information System (MIS) course had a lab where tutors were available to assist with any problems with material presented in class or with the assigned homework. If available, it is beneficial to utilize teaching assistants (TA) to help you understand difficult concepts presented in class. A TA's main role is to help with homework/concept problems that students may have. Likewise, engaging the professor directly during their respective office hours not only helps develop rapport but will also help you when it comes to meeting with them (i.e., showing them your class notes, "putting a face to a name"). Consequently they will be more than likely to assist you. As music artist and social media personality DJ Khaled would say this is a "major key."

It is also important to ensure that you are always above reproach with respect to not plagiarizing or cheating on exams and assignments. Academic dishonesty is extremely difficult to recover from. One way to make sure you never run into this problem is to follow assignment instructions but not look at any examples; in other words do your work from scratch. Also make sure to use the various plagiarism checker websites to help make sure you are not using someone else's material. When in doubt, over cite your work. It is better to be safe than labeled a cheater.

Generally speaking, I did quite well on exams, but there were some exam scores that were in the B to B+ range. Taking advantage of every opportunity to earn points such as homework assignments, extra credit and class participation helped to boost my overall GPA and made it possible for me to graduate with honors with a degree in Economics and a minor in Business. Had I not taken advantage of some of the aforementioned strategies to garner additional points, my GPA would have been significantly lower! Although it's beyond a student-athlete's control, it's good to be aware that there are some professors who employ what is commonly known as a "Bell Curve" to adjust grades within a course depending on the difficulty of the exams and how well other classmates perform.

I've touched upon homework and attendance but one of the items to which I wish to pay particular attention and which I have mentioned previously is "extra credit." Extra credit does not literally mean "extra," but it's more like in athletics when you have those optional practices that are deemed mandatory by your fellow teammates. **Extra in terms of academics should really be mandatory**, as it is the easiest way to create that cushion come exam time. In the analogy with athletics, just like you don't want to lose out on a rep, giveaway points, or runs, the same mentality must be taken with extra credit. One never knows what percentage point will bring a C+ to a B- or a B+ to an A-. That's why it is crucial to get as many points during the course of the semester.

For example, in my marketing course there were a number of extra credit opportunities and they were done by taking a survey for the department. My 81 on an exam quickly turned into a 95 because the extra credit that I earned was worth 14 points! THAT'S A BIG TIME BOOST! My point is, utilize this extra credit opportunity, as it can help boost your GPA. Combining your homework and extra credit are very good ways to boost your GPA. To reiterate, collegiate athletes possess certain intangibles (discipline, hard-working, ability to perform under pressure) that other may not. However, what athletes sometimes lack is the GPA to go along with these intangibles. When it comes time to join the working world, it is advantageous having this perfect marriage of a high GPA and a student-athlete's inherent skills as these will separate you from the rest, identify you as a person of value, and contribute to your success.

8th Inning

GPA & Academic Assistance

"Without a struggle, there can be no progress."
-Frederick Douglass

Let's look at why it is essential to take your schooling seriously. While growing up, guardians provide for you, care for you, and in return, only ask of you to behave properly and do your best in school. In life and in school there is a certain level of "give a S#*%" that is required. **If you apply effort and care you will not bring home below average grades.** Certainly there are courses that are tougher than others but if you truly do your best, follow the principles and techniques outlined in this book you will be successful.

In the investment world they talk about diversification and not "putting all your eggs in one basket." Many athletes work tirelessly to become professional athletes, not only to fulfill their own goals, but also to support and take care of those who have continuously made sacrifices that have allowed them to compete everyday in their respective sports. We have all seen the Twitter posts or bios that state "Working like I do so you don't have to." However, it is important to realize that there are many ways to provide for yourself and your respective family.

As athletes, the opportunity to obtain valuable work experience that employers look for when hiring is more difficult due to your more extensive time demands than those of an everyday college student.

College coaches frequently ask members of their teams to report early during summer, winter and spring breaks be it for either athletic or academic reasons. Therefore, time demands for student-athletes can be significantly more challenging than their non-athlete peers.

A higher than average GPA demonstrates to an employer that you have a number of desirable traits including: being hardworking, driven, and competent. This helps separate you from others by achieving an impressive GPA while playing a high level college sport with all of its associated time constraints. Additionally, many employers look for individuals who can bring qualities such as the ability to work with in a team environment and the ability to work under pressure; common characteristics of being a collegiate athlete. If there is one thing that I deem a "controllable" it is your GPA as only you can ensure that it is kept at a high level. It is interesting to note that there is a strong relationship between GPA and higher earnings (Marte, 2014) so be sure to do everything possible to maintain a high GPA.

Depending on the collegiate sport, there can be a limited number of scholarships allotted per team. For instance, NCAA Division I baseball teams are allotted 11.7 full scholarships to distribute among all their players (normally there are approximately 30 to 40 players per team). Therefore, there are very few "Full Rides" from an athletic scholarship standpoint in many "non-revenue generating sports." A college education is very expensive. One way to offset a portion of this cost is by qualifying for some sort of academic scholarship along with whatever portion is allocated through the athletic scholarship.

As a graduating high school student-athlete you are able to make yourself more marketable to college coaches if you have a high GPA and SAT/ACT scores. This creates opportunities to obtain academic funds, which will offset some of the limitation of athletic scholarship funding. This is also the case for student-athletes who are looking to transfer from two-year junior colleges to four-year universities. There are a multitude of scholarships and tuition waivers available at all colleges/universities. It is important to constantly research what is available in order to see if you either qualify for or can apply for such additional financial support.

For example, at public institutions the cost of tuition and even fees differs for in-state and out-of-state students. However, if one is an out of state student there are ways to qualify for an "out-of-state" tuition waiver. One of the ways this can be done is by maintaining a certain GPA as a scholarship athlete. This was the case for me at the University of Houston as I was on scholarship as an "out-of-state" international student. I worked hard to maintain a GPA high enough to qualify for an "out-of-state tuition waiver." Obviously, obtaining a tuition waiver greatly diminished the remaining amount that my parents had to pay for my overall education as I was on a partial athletic scholarship. Each school is different and it is important to ask individuals at your respective institution how you can qualify for these waivers. Every little bit helps.

It is important to ask questions and see what other opportunities there may be but it's a lot harder to do so if you don't build credibility and in this case it's done through your GPA. The moral of the story here is "**the higher your GPA is, the more opportunities you will have.**"

9th Inning

Memorization, Maturation, Test Taking Tips

"Education is the most powerful weapon which you can use to change the world." -Nelson Mandela

Education is part of a maturation process. Some people are just naturally gifted and for whatever reason school comes easier to them. However, for the majority, including myself, school is more difficult and it's necessary to find your own learning style that will lead you to success. Various tips outlined throughout this book should help you achieve your goals but be sure to find strategies that work for you. It wasn't until my freshman year of college that I found out what worked for me. At this point I made a conscious decision to not be just average anymore. Memorization is something that helped me in this regard.

I have always had a good memory. In school, problems on exams, tests, and assignments often dealt with conceptual issues. I didn't always grasp these concepts the way the teacher taught them, which would then lead me to become frustrated and confused. Upon entering college I began to realize that if I just memorized steps that led me to the correct answer, regardless if I understood it or not, I would still get some credit as opposed to just saying "I don't understand this so I won't worry about it." One key thing to remember is even if you don't know or don't think you know the answer to a question on an exam it is best to write something down as opposed to leaving it blank because you may receive partial credit. Also, when I began to memorize steps, it began to help me make sense of certain concepts that I previously was not able to grasp. **An associated benefit of this memorization technique allowed me to really bear down and focus on my various subjects. It's no different than memorizing a playbook or studying game film.**

Another important change to my studying techniques helped me improve my success when taking exams. I changed my approach from only studying what I thought would be on an exam and thereby studying in effect 85% of the information in an attempt to get what would at best yield an 85 on the exam. If you have thoughts such as: "I wonder if this will be on the exam, should I study it" chances are you should. Otherwise, on the day of the exam, you will be met with a number of unwelcomed surprises. Frustration will stem from not having seen some of the material, to seeing the material but not knowing enough about it, and consequently not having learned it.

During college I studied 100% of the information knowing that I would be better prepared for exams and minimize the amount of material I had never seen before. Setting a goal of studying the material in its entirety helped raise my exam averages significantly with many in the 90s. Also, by studying all of the material you will have a **sharper focus on what your professors have presented throughout the semester regarding potential content of the exam.**

I chose to mark information that I knew would be important with **asterisks or a box, so it was easy to find and focus on when studying.**

Also, **exam reviews are extremely beneficial whether they take place in class or are sent to students via an e-mailed document.** In my case, math was always a difficult subject, especially when it came to concepts. Once I began college, many of my math courses provided practice exams prior to the exams (usually extra credit as well). These practice exams normally allayed any of my fears going into the exams, as they were reflective of the exam material. Once again I would memorize steps to help me out. In summation, preparation is very important and as Russell Wilson NFL quarterback of the Seattle Seahawks noted "*The separation is in the preparation* (Wyche, 2014)."

I was enrolled in an American history class during my junior year of college and the exam review stated that we would be given six essay topics, of which three would be directly taken from the exam review. Six separate essays was a lot of material and I had amassed 25 pages worth of notes. If I would have adopted a study approach that many college students take of studying and cramming the night before, I don't know if I could have succeeded or remembered all of the information. In short, I preferred to study well in advance.

At the University of Houston our baseball coach Todd Whitting frequently reminded his players to keep "doing a little a lot." This related perfectly to my habit of studying well in advance. To continue on this theme of not leaving things to the last minute, it's important to break down the material night by night.

For example, if you have 10 pages of notes (20 front and back) and it's Sunday with an exam scheduled for the upcoming Friday, you would study, understand, and memorize two pages worth of material a day. Starting on Sunday you would memorize two pages. On the Monday, you would go over and make sure that you have learned/memorized Sunday's material and then learn and memorize two new pages. This strategy would continue each day until Thursday whereby a review of all previously studied material would occur along with 2 new pages for that day. By Thursday you will have covered and fully studied all 20 pages inside out. Another side benefit is that this study habit allows you to visit the professor during office hours to ask questions on any concepts that you may not grasp particularly well as you are preparing in advance.

During the fall semester of my senior year I was enrolled in a rigorous 18-hour, predominantly upper level, economics and business course load. During this semester the only way I was able to find success with the various time demands of baseball and weights, was to employ the aforementioned study techniques of consistent study rather than cramming at the last minute. **As a student-athlete, regardless of being in or out of season, it is essential to get ahead with your homework and assignments. This allows you to ask questions of professors as well as take advantage of practice tests, tutors and exam reviews.** With respect to memorization techniques, if you are stuck on a certain formula or you are having an "I can't remember the word but I know the meaning" moment, think of a short acronym or associate a particular phrase with it. For example, for a simple supply and demand graph in economics, the best way I could remember which curve went where on a basic graph was by writing the word *sUPpply (using a* capital UP) this way as this curve went up and conversely the D in Demand is associated with the word down as demand goes down.

Another memorization tool that I used was having another person hold my study notes and quiz me on the material. If I had difficulty with a particular concept I would have whoever was quizzing me tell me the answer and then come back to it later on during that review session. It is important to mix up the order when you are being quizzed as topics on exams are not going to be in the same order you studied and this will truly test your ability to retain the material.

Extra Innings
10th Inning

Compete Mode

> *"Competing at the highest level is the greatest test of one's character." Russell Mark*

There is no substitute for hard work, end of story. Like anything else in life, if you want to be successful at something you have to work hard. Nothing worth having is ever handed to you. As a collegiate athlete you understand what it is like to work your hardest and to compete at one of the highest levels. Tom Herman, former Head Football Coach at the University of Houston, has said "go 1-0." To me this means winning, dominating whatever task is at hand, be it a game, a weight training rep or doing well on a certain play against a particular opponent. When an individual is in their "Athletic Compete Mode" (ACM), it allows for them to find success when the odds aren't necessarily in their favour and shatter seemingly unbreakable records. Even if your technique isn't fundamentally sound or you may not be the smoothest at something, your ACM kicks in and can lead to extraordinary success. I challenge you to tap into your ACM that is naturally present within competitive student-athletes and apply it to your academics. There are several benefits to using this mental state, namely, it fulfills and satisfies ones self, in the same way as it satisfies and brings fulfillment when one has defeated another opponent. With respect to academics you are competing not only against yourself, your previous exams/assignments but also your classmates. Once you have tapped into this "compete mode" it will allow you to put in your best effort, not just sprinting to the finish line but running through it, not just completing the assignment because it's due but dominating it, and putting your signature on it. In addition, when you are completely locked into this ACM and apply it to academics you will start to figure things out "on the fly." For instance, this will help when it comes time to take an exam that you have worked hard to prepare for but, for some reason, something just does not compute.

On exam day, one question on the exam may lead into another and if you are able to make a link and breakthrough because you are in this mental state, you are more likely to do well. Being in this "compete mode" you will have an easier time finding the correct answers.

11th Inning

School Is What You Make Of It

"If you change the way you look at things, the things you look at change." -Wayne Dyer

Choosing which school to attend is a big decision. You can do all your due diligence but there is no substitute for experiencing the school. At this point some will love it; others will hate it, and a couple months after, your feeling may change once again. After all, your experience is what you make of it. You may have a demanding coach, a tough academic program, or a social life that is nonexistent. These are all part of being a student-athlete.

You can point fingers, blame others all day long, but only you have a choice as to how you react to certain situations. You can choose to get involved; you can choose to take pride in your school, in your community, your sport, your classes. There are a variety of programs within the athletic department and outside of it that can help you become involved, whether it's going to various college sporting events, doing volunteer work, or joining a Student-Athlete Advisory Committee (SAAC). These are just a few examples of programs to help you get involved. The only complaint that I've ever heard from someone who "got involved" was that they had too much on their plate and needed to cut back. This came from the same person who was miserable throughout their whole first year and didn't start finding complete happiness until they got involved. Oftentimes as athletes we are put on a pedestal, and people may believe that we aren't affected by the same things that others are. When you are walking by any student (athlete or not), be sure to smile and say to them "what's up", hold the door for them. Through simple gestures you may just make someone's day because you never know when someone may have just been chewed out at practice/work or just received a poor grade on an exam.

12th Inning

The Company You Keep

"Surround yourself with only people who are going to lift you higher." –Oprah Winfrey

At Salt Lake Community College our baseball team rule was "don't do anything that will embarrass your family name, the school, the program and those who have helped you get to where you are at." Not only does this apply to your respective sport and social life but to academics as well. If you are going to put your signature or name on something, make sure it's your best work as your signature represents YOU.

You are Measured by the Company You Keep, So Represent Yourself, Your School, and Your Family Well. What do you want to represent and how do you want to be viewed are both questions that you must consider when faced with various decisions that will lead to shaping your brand or image. Furthermore, as a student-athlete you are constantly under a microscope. A general rule of thumb is to not associate yourself with those who don't have as much to lose as you do. Growing up my parents would always say, you are judged by the company you keep. This never rang more true than when I attended college, I was faced with many situations that could have compromised my efforts and career.

You do not want to associate yourself with individuals who are so called "liabilities." In sports we talk about "controlling what you can control" as this will lead to more success and less anxiety. If you do this you will be able to create an environment that will lead to more favourable results no matter the scenario. Be careful with the clothes you wear because your image/reputation is at stake. Be sure not to wear another university's logo or clothing on campus as it is disrespectful and an unwritten rule among students and even more so among student-athletes. At the same time understand that as an athlete you represent your team and the school's athletic program. Wearing team issued apparel brings attention to not only you, but to your team, athletic department and school. This could be beneficial if you are participating in charity work or acting in a positive manner. You must be aware that you represent your team and can harm your school's image should you conduct yourself inappropriately. Taking this one step further, in today's day and age, with the prevalence and accessibility of cellphones, cameras, and video along with various social media platforms, there is the potential for possible behaviour to go viral. This is twofold, for one this could lead to an amazing opportunity as a student-athlete in that you can build your brand and image. An example of this is Marcus Stroman (professional athlete, Duke Graduate) and his effective use of social media more specifically, his twitter account. He has a rather large following of more than 200 thousand people and he utilizes this platform daily from motivational, positive quotes and tweets, to his trademarked "HDMH" which he has built a brand around. Another thing that it can do is damage you. One example of a social media, technology catastrophe was of a football player who may have lost a lot of money due to the things that were leaked on him on draft day.

Always treat everyone with respect and make sure that you do not associate yourself with individuals who are likely to commit illegal or unethical acts. This is also very important when it comes to social media usage and Twitter/Facebook postings. Be more social media savvy and ensure that you don't post anything that can potentially embarrass yourself, your school, or your family. There are countless examples of student-athletes who lose scholarships because of what they post on social media.

College and the atmosphere that accompanies it is fun and exciting, but also presents scenarios where student-athletes are forced to make decisions that their non-athlete peers may not have to make. As a student-athlete you are not able to live the same lifestyle as a regular student. Your team and schedule demands much more. It is not fair to yourself or your teammates to be going out the night before games. In saying this, when it is permissible to go out make sure that you are able to get to and from your destination safely. There are apps that will be able to get you to where you need to go or you can have a designated driver. Take care of yourself and your teammates. There is no value in putting your life and the lives of others in jeopardy.

The Golden Tools For A Student-Athlete

"Become addicted to constant and never-ending self-improvement." –Anthony J. D'Angelo

The following are a set of tools that have been core to my success as a student-athlete and for the sake of being precise are outlined in a bulleted fashion:

TOOL #1 -COMPLIANCE

- ✓ Always check your school policies and your scholarship award letters, but generally athletic scholarships are for one year. Recently, the Power 5 conferences [Atlantic Coast Conference (ACC), Big Ten Conference (B1G), Big 12 Conference, Pac-12 Conference and Southeastern Conference (SEC)] voted on legislation that states that a coach cannot revoke a scholarship because of athletic performance and thereby guaranteeing scholarships for four-year. This is not the case across all conferences and therefore **it is imperative to remember that being a scholarship/walk on athlete on a team is not a right but rather a privilege.** Be sure to not give a coach an excuse to revoke your scholarship or your position on the team due to poor grades, bad attitude, off field behavior or a "violation of team rules".
- ✓ If you are on scholarship and an item is not directly covered, but you feel as though it should be (e.g., buying a clicker), it is important to keep

the receipt and talk to an individual within the athletic department to see if it can be reimbursed.

- ✓ There are various ways to earn money while being an athlete in college. It is critical that you check to ensure that any revenue producing activity you engage in is done in accordance with the Compliance department's rules and regulations. There are several methods by which you can make extra money such as working concession stands at various sporting events or working at sports camps at your respective school. Another way to make money is by going to your school's website and looking for surveys/tests/studies that certain departments, such as the Psychology Department, are offering. In many cases, you can be paid for participating in such research studies.
- ✓ While participating in sports at the collegiate level there are certain rules and regulations you must adhere to whether you agree with them or not. It is critical that you ask questions about rules you may not be clear about. For instance, ask compliance about a certain rule or a nutritionist about a certain product. I have often heard people state that, "your college career isn't worth $30 on a banned substance in a product you bought off the shelf." It is better to be safe than sorry in this instance. First and foremost you should always reach out to your school's compliance officers and school nutritionists but there are also helpful links on the internet: **http://www.ncaa.org/compliance**

TOOL #2 – THE SELF

✓ The importance of having a person, persons, or group that you can go to for anything is critical in college. You are going to be faced with multiple situations athletically, in the classroom, and in life throughout college that will require you to seek guidance and a sense of clarity that you alone can't bring to yourself. You know who these people are. In my case, I was able to develop relationships with different people, which allowed me to draw on different types of expertise depending on the subject. This "person" for me changed depending on the situation. I was able to go to my assistant baseball coach at SLCC for anything, my Mom, my Dad, my brother, my girlfriend and my strength coach at Houston, Lee Fiocchi. The situation dictates the person in whom you need to confide.

TOOL #3 - "RESPECT YOUR PEERS"

✓ Respect the seniors on your team. They are your most valuable resources on campus, and they want you to succeed. There will be some duties that you will have to do that may seem annoying, but guess what, everyone was once a freshman and had to do the very same things. These seniors are a valuable resource and will be able to answer questions and hopefully provide guidance on questions regarding school, sport and life. Furthermore, when going into a four-year school or a junior college "close the yearbook." No one wants to hear about your high school statistics because none of that matters anymore. **Respect**

is not earned by what you say, but rather by what you do.

- ✓ It is important to be honest, accountable, and communicate with your team, your academic staff, and your coaches. If you are going to be late to something, let someone know to give them a heads up. It is always better to be proactive as opposed to reactive. In fact, be early for class, practice, and appointments: this way you show a level of respect that will make you stand out.

- ✓ Respect your roommate. If you are living in a dorm there will be times where you are going to be all up in each other's space and butting heads, but make sure cooler heads prevail. My roommates have turned out to be some of my best friends and that is in large part due to me remaining true to the person I am and them doing the same.

TOOL #4 - KNOW YOUR COURSES

- ✓ For junior college (JUCO) transfers, different credits transfer depending on where your JUCO is located. For instance, I went to JUCO in Utah and then transferred to Houston. The Houston education system has different requirements and course codes. As long as you take "real" course work you shouldn't have an issue with being able to transfer. The issue will lie in whether or not "ALL" of your credits will be accepted and be deemed transferable. This is because course codes and requirements differ from institution to institution. What you can do, and what I had to do, was to petition for my course work to be approved by the University of Houston. During this petitioning process I needed a course description and a copy of the syllabus. There were two courses from my JUCO for which I did not have the syllabus but thanks to the relationships I had built with the faculty members at my JUCO I was able to obtain them. This leads me to my next point.

✓ Keep your course work. All of it: from the syllabus, to every homework assignment, to each exam given back. You are never going to know when you'll have to draw on the material or show a professor if he/she inputs the incorrect grade. It helps especially in upper level courses if you need to brush up on a concept from a previous introductory course. If I hadn't kept the work/documents that I did at my JUCO I would not have been able to petition for all of the courses that I did.

✓ Being a student-athlete is tough. If you don't have time to get something done, it means you are not managing your time properly. I wrote this book during baseball season, with a full course load, and still gave my undivided attention to my sport and my courses. Find a way, just like you do in your sport, to execute what is asked of you but also carry this "efficient" mentality outside your respective sport. **A good rule of thumb is "if you are not ahead you are behind."**

- ✓ It is possible to get ahead in the classroom with respect to your degree or "catch up" by taking courses in the summer/winter semesters. It can be on your dime or you can see if the school/athletic department will pay for it.

- ✓ In terms of studying, I always found it best to re-write my class notes for the exam as opposed to memorizing straight from the notes I had taken in class. Not only did it allow for me to process the material once again but it separated my exam notes from my class notes. Some may prefer to study straight from their class notes and others from their computers.

- ✓ Depending on what your major coursework entails, you may run into issues as to the type of computer you need to use. Specific operating systems work better for certain assignments and majors. It is important to understand what enables you to complete an assignment with the greatest ease and success. Schools have computer labs and on top of that some offer discounts or free software so it is important to look into this.

- ✓ When you are studying don't let the negative thoughts of looking at the clock and thinking "dang I've only been here for one hour" or "I have been studying for so long" occupy your mind. You know how long you need to study; you have to be conscious that you are not left with the empty feeling that you haven't studied enough. Don't limit yourself, just like in the weight room finish each rep/each set/each page/each note.

- ✓ If you feel like class is dragging along, ask questions, and get involved in the discussion. Not only will you learn more but also it will make class more enjoyable and time go by faster. My Dad always told me to be a "sponge" meaning you can always learn something from those around you. There is no better way to learn than by asking questions.

- ✓ There is no statistic or percentage that can be placed on the value of asking questions and "being a sponge." This learning can be done through listening to one speak but you can even get more knowledge and more depth to certain topics by asking tactful questions. Don't ever be afraid to say I don't know, as honesty is always important. Asking questions allows you to be in the know as opposed to the unknown. The more well versed you are on a variety of issues will allow for you to speak on many different levels, to many different people and enable you to become a more well-rounded individual.

- ✓ Whether you are struggling or not in a course, a good tool to utilize is *reading* the material before class. This allows for a different level of familiarity with what will be covered and will aid in the understanding of the coursework.

TOOL #5 - NO LIMITS TO SUCCESS

- ✓ Don't ever let anyone put limits on you. I was 5 ft 8 inches and 145 lbs in high school. In fact, I was laughed at repeatedly for saying I wanted to play professional baseball and was told countless times

I would never play at a Division I school, let alone one that was ranked in the top 10. **There are certain things in this world that people can't quantify or measure and those are: how big one's heart, drive, and determination are.** There is a specific person and thing that holds the key to your destiny and the path you take in life and that person is **You** and that thing is your **Attitude.**

TOOL #6 - CHALLENGE YOURSELF

✓ I took Intermediate Micro-economics in a condensed summer semester. The professor stated that it was going to be a very difficult course and that at his previous school they would not allow students to take it during the summer. At first this shook me, as I was a transfer student and didn't know what I was getting myself into. Nonetheless, I was not going to let what this professor said define me or apply to me. Just like in sports I was going to prove him wrong. Furthermore, as a student-athlete you have a chance to have a portion of, if not all, your schooling paid for. It would be foolish if you did not take full advantage of this. In this instance, taking full advantage means getting the "best bang for your buck." If you can handle it, get an engineering degree, a finance degree, a biology degree. Don't settle for the perceived "easy" degrees. Furthermore, throughout your collegiate career you may have a "redshirt" year where you don't use a year of your eligibility. Don't look at this as a setback; rather look at it as an opportunity. Make sure you stay on track with your schooling and take care of whatever needs to be done to get back on track athletically (i.e., weight room, rehabilitation, polishing your athletic skill set). If you are a scholarship athlete this redshirt year provides an opportunity for you to graduate in four years, come back for a fifth year and have a masters degree paid for. Talk about getting bang for your buck!

TOOL #7 - DON'T BE SHY

- ✓ Sometimes administrative or grading errors can be made on exams whereby there is a tally error in overall points and it's critical that you calculate all of them so that they match your grade. If you believe you have earned a better grade than what is shown, respectfully ask and provide a justification for your query. During the spring semester of my junior year my calculations of my grades didn't match the grades the professors inputted into the UH system. I immediately got in touch with them and discovered there was a discrepancy in the system. It is important that you do this because just as in sport, you never know which point/stroke/run/ will win you a game. The same is applied to school as you never know which point on an exam or an assignment will take you from a B+ to an A-.

TOOL #8 - UPS & DOWNS

- ✓ If you are an international student keep in mind that the US dollar in relation to your home currency can fluctuate. When I first started college the US dollar and Canadian dollar were relatively at par, meaning 1 US dollar was the equivalent to 1 Canadian dollar. By my senior year at Houston for every 1 US dollar it would cost my family $1.40 Canadian dollar. This could affect your cost for schooling if you don't budget accordingly.

- ✓ **Throughout the course of the semester you are going to have ups and downs and it is critical to stay the course.** During my college career there were times I would calculate my GPA and it scared me as it was not what I wanted. This would seem to light a fire under me and I would then usually outdo my previous semester GPA high.

- ✓ An area that has become more important within athletic departments and the school altogether are career development services. It is important for a student-athlete to utilize these services, as they help with the transition from collegiate life to the working world. Staff in these departments will help with resume building, offer workshops on making the transition to life after college (e.g., interview workshops), make student-athletes aware of potential job opportunities and connect them with previous student-athlete and institution alums.

- ✓ There will be a number of instances in your college career when your core values, beliefs, goals, and ideology will be tested. Now that you are entering or are enrolled in college you should know what is right and what is wrong. If all of these things just mentioned are "good" it is very important that you not stray away from them. I will tell you from first-hand experience there is nothing more rewarding than being told by others that they appreciate you for simply being who you are. Not faking it to be someone you are not. Over the years as you stick to your core foundation you will weed out those who are not needed in your life and retain those who are going to be lasting friends.

✓ One thing to keep in mind is the value of what is at stake. In the world of sports many deem that worth is determined by the number of zeros associated with an opportunity or the amount of playing time you get. In collegiate sports you are playing and working towards a greater goal. It doesn't matter if you are a walk on or a scholarship player. Each and every one of us has aspirations to start every game, match, event, and to play professionally (if your sport has a professional league). It is important to keep in mind that whatever your role is on a given game day you need to be the best teammate you can be. That's not to say that you have to be happy about not playing and have high expectations for yourself but there is no benefit in being negative or not helping those around you. No one likes being around someone with negative energy and this can isolate you from the rest of the team. Furthermore, not only do the players notice this behaviour and talk about it but so do the coaches and this can hurt your career. I have been on both ends of the spectrum of starting and not starting. When you can't contribute on the field, find ways to contribute off the field. At the end of the day, the entire team gets the acknowledgment and the rings when a title is won.

TOOL #9 - FUEL

- ✓ One issue that you will always encounter no matter the amount of "unlimited food or snacks" you get as an athlete is access to food. Just when you think you've bought enough or eaten enough, you haven't. One of the best tools that I didn't utilize nearly enough is the ability to freeze food. Devote a Sunday afternoon each week or every two weeks to make food and freeze it in Tupperware. My Mom is an incredible chef: when she would come visit me at school and would make Shepherd's Pie and other favorites, I would freeze them and eat over a couple of weeks. Two rules of thumb, no tin foil in the microwave, it won't end well and always check to make sure you shut off the oven or stove before you leave.

- ✓ **Breakfast** is the most important meal of the day. You may have workouts at early hours, so one very easy way to get a substantial meal in is by cracking an egg in a microwave safe bowl and putting a paper towel over it for 45 seconds while at the same time putting a piece of toast or an English muffin in the toaster. You can repeat this process for however many times you want and in a matter of minutes you'll be out the door with a full stomach. Get creative, put a slice of cheese on it. Also, having hard-boiled eggs prepared is very effective when it comes to utilizing the short amount time you have in the morning.

- ✓ It is a necessity to constantly have snacks with you. If I felt sluggish or not attentive enough in class, I would reach for the snacks kept in my backpack to curb my appetite. If I was lacking focus, it was often in large part due to my hunger.

- ✓ Staying hydrated is especially important. As a student-athlete, a reusable water bottle was one of the best purchases I had ever made. You tax your body unlike anyone else and without proper hydration you will not be able to perform to your fullest capability on the field, in the classroom or during your daily tasks.

TOOL #10 - MONEY

- ✓ A hot topic in sports is money management. You hear horror stories about how athletes lose all of their money, but I am here to tell you that it doesn't have to be this way. It is in your best interest to utilize a budget. This can be done through an Excel template or apps that you can download from the web. This will not only better serve you for later in life when you have a larger income but will help you keep track of all of your inflows and outflows. An example of a budget can be seen on the next page.

- ✓ In fact, as a scholarship athlete and depending on how much money the school, your parents, and the government disperses to you, there is a chance that you may have money left over. In this scenario, it would be wise to meet with a financial planner and not just "save" this money but allow for this extra money to grow by investing it wisely.

SAMPLE SPENDING TRACKER

Date	Groceries	Restaurant	Pleasure	Grooming	School	Gas	Totals
Actual	$ -	$ -	$ -	$ -	$ -	$ -	$ -
Budget	$ 200.00	$ 100.00	$ 40.00	$ 30.00	$ 25.00	$ 30.00	$ 600.00
Over/Under	$ 200.00	$ 100.00		$ 30.00	$ 25.00	$ 30.00	-$ 600.00

- ✓ Once you've completed your undergraduate degree you may be thinking of graduate school. However, graduate school can be very expensive and one way to offset the cost is to become a **Graduate Assistant** where your employment can help pay for school. If you want to remain at the same school where you just completed your undergraduate degree, it is important to **ask questions** to find out if this opportunity will present itself. Also, there are various links where you can find out about positions offered at other schools (e.g., http://ncaamarket.ncaa.org/jobs).

- ✓ Buy a watch. Not only will this aid in helping you stay off your phone during class to "check the time" but also many of your exams will be timed and will understandably not allow you to use any electronic devices. Having a watch will allow you to keep track of the time. Also, a watch is a great tool when you are working out, whether that is when you go for a run, or if your strength coach asks you to keep track of how long it takes you to work out. Furthermore, it brings about a sense of professionalism.

TOOL #11 - YOUR BODY IS YOUR BUSINESS

- ✓ Sometimes you won't understand why but just like in sports if your coach tells you to do something a certain way you just have to trust him: in other words, be open minded and coachable. Same thing in school. Read instructions, follow instructions and give maximum effort.

- ✓ Athletic trainers play a key role in your performance as an athlete. As an athlete your body will be challenged and taxed. With the nature of sport and its demands, it is possible that you will endure an injury or some nicks on your body. It is important to communicate with your trainers but also to know the difference between having an injury and just being sore. Furthermore, if you ever become ill it is important to not only reach out to your coaches but also to your trainers to find out how you should go about getting the necessary treatment. At the University of Houston we had doctors come in on Monday and Wednesday mornings. Be appreciative of the work that the doctors and trainers are doing for you; they play an important role in keeping you on the field.

- ✓ Sticking with the theme of your body being taxed, it is critical that you are able to get enough sleep and recovery. This is important for both your performance in sport but also in the classroom. Try to take a nap during the day to recharge if you are unable to get a good night's rest.

- ✓ There will be various times when you might not feel well throughout the course of a semester. You'll notice that during exams your body will feel depleted and this will be accentuated even more so while your sport is in season. The most common illness that I came down with was the common cold. The best advice that I can give you that helped me out immensely, other than taking medicine, was buying a few boxes of aloe vera tissues. Whether it was because it soothed my nose or in turn put me in a better mood. It made the cold more bearable and shortened its life span.

- ✓ An athlete's wardrobe consists of spandex, compressions, sports bras, sweats, hoodies, mid calf sport socks and Dri FITS. Although these articles of clothing will be appropriate for about 90% of your time in college, there are times when you will require other outerwear. Whether it be a presentation, going on a date, a banquet, a donor dinner, an interview, or even team travel, it is **essential that you have outfits that are business casual and business formal.** An example of business casual for women would be: skirt, slacks, a blouse or a dress shirt, closed toe shoes for business formal. For men, business casual includes a dress shirt or a polo with khakis/dress pants accompanied by dress shoes/cowboy boots (#AsSeenInTexas) whereas business formal includes a suit and tie.

TOOL #12 - SCHEDULING CLASSES

- ✓ Although you may have academic advisors help you schedule your classes, make sure to take into account your practice schedule. First, you have to make sure there aren't any conflicts. Second, from my personal experience, it isn't wise to schedule a very challenging/demanding course right after practice, as you may be very tired. This is once again why it is so critical to stay on top of your scheduling, so you are able to get the proper nutrition to be able to perform.

- ✓ At the end of the day, you may not have any other options, as that may be the only time slot that a required course is offered. Similar to competition, when times are tough you have to find a way to perform and make it work.

The following is a speech that I was asked to prepare and give in front of over one hundred graduating seniors, university faculty members, athletic faculty members and donors at the Senior breakfast on May 9th, 2016 at the Athletic Alumni Centre at The University of Houston.

Senior Breakfast Speech

By Robert Grilli

A Houston Cougar. When I Googled the meaning behind the mascot, the animal, the nickname that our university represents it came up with the definition of a "large American wild cat with a plain tawny to grayish coat." Although I understand that this is depicting the animal and its coat, this definition somewhat frustrated me, as the word plain has no business being in the same sentence as Cougar, let alone a Houston Cougar. Before looking at this I had always thought this animal was defined as an intelligent, unique and powerful cat much more akin to the one our university represents. However, what no definition, no webpage search can speak to is what it truly means to be a Houston cougar until you have lived it.

A Houston Cougar embodies a number of things but if I were to choose one word it would be CULTURE:

When I say culture I'm not talking strictly from a wins and losses standpoint-don't get me wrong, we win a lot around here and will continue to do so; but what I'm referencing about culture is the members and attitude that form the very being that it is. The sense of community, support and open lines of communication truly separates UH. I don't know if it's a written rule somewhere but each coach, professor and employee seems to abide by an open door policy, a smile followed by a how are you and y'all doing, a hold the door when they see you are a few feet away. What makes this even more special is in athletics it can be a very cutthroat industry but here at UH this openness, this sense of community is truly what separates and allows for unprecedented growth and continued success.

This success is not only seen in each athletes respective sport but the very reason we are gathered here today is because of the success we've found in the classroom. The professors here at UH are special in their own right for their constant support and willingness to work with the unique schedules us student-athletes face. Take for instance, Dr. Bott, who I believe is in attendance today and if I were a betting man he's wearing red. His tremendous passion, hard work love and support for the university and athletics is a microcosm for what this university is about. And he is just one of the many examples of fine professors this great university has. For this, I would like to extend a thank you to every athletic department staff, to each coach, each trainer and each professor who has empowered and enabled each of us to get to where we are today.

Furthermore, this culture here at UH is a family. As an athlete many of the individuals in this room are living away from what society would deem their "immediate family." When you attend UH as a student-athlete you are constantly surrounded by your new family who quickly turn into your "immediate family." This family extends through various sports teams and I know that without this family we would not be here today. When a prospective student-athlete is in the recruiting process and mulling over the decision of whether to attend a school one of the biggest questions is whether it works financially. In the world of sports many deem that something's worth is determined by the number of zeros associated with an opportunity. At UH the true value lies in being a Cougar. Over the years you see those who get weeded out but the individuals sitting here today are entering a new chapter in their life with the values and traits that embody a Cougar; accountability, excellence, loyalty, inclusivity and integrity.

Today we gather as brothers and sisters to celebrate and reflect on the end of one of the many journeys that we will take in our lifetime. Each and every single person in this room has authored their own story, which has allowed for them to take a path enabling them to get to this day. This path has been ripe with trials and tribulations inherent to being a student-athlete both on and off the field. Some have been roaming this athletic alumni center for 2 years others for 4 or 5 but no matter the case this month or in the next few months will mark a historic achievement in our lives. Some of the individuals in this room will be the first time college graduates in their family and others will be following in one's footsteps and become a legacy here at the University of Houston.

No matter where we came from, no matter what walk of life we will embark on, we are here today to celebrate something that we will forever have in common. Something that I am honoured to share with each and everyone of you and that is the honour of graduating as a Student-Athlete from The University of Houston as a Cougar and as a Champion for Life. *Go Coogs.*

Year in Review:

Goals at the end of the year:

Which of your goals have you completed? If you didn't achieve them, -why and how are you going to move forward?

ACADEMIC GOALS

(e.g., Achieve 4.0 GPA, Academic All Region, Dean's list, Graduate)

ATHLETIC GOALS

____

(e.g., Earn a starting position, Win a Conference/National Championship, various others)

SOCIAL GOALS

(e.g., Surround yourself with great friends who support you through the good and bad).

References

Baptiste, B. (2003). *Journey Into Power.* Touchstone; Reprint edition.

D'Angelo, A.J. (n.d.) http://thinkexist.com

Dyer, W. (September, 2009) http://drwaynedyer.com

Khlaed, DJ. (2016). **https://twitter.com/djkhaled**

Mandela, N. in. (2012). Steadman, G. & Blanchard, K. *Leader, Know Thyself.* Pearson.

Mark, R. (n.d.) http://workedia.com

Marte, J. (May 20, 2014). Here's how much your high school grades predict your future salary. The Washington Post. Retrieved from: **https://www.washingtonpost.com/news/wonk/wp/2014/05/20/heres-how-much-your-high-school-grades-predict-how-much-you-make-today/**

Phelps, M. (n.d.) teamunify.com

Rankin, S., Merson, D., Sorgen, C.H., McHale, I., Loya, K., Oseguera, L. (2011). Student-Athlete Climate Study (SACS) Final Report, Center for the Study of Higher Education, The Pennsylvania State University

Rather, D. in. Swainston, T. (2008). *Effective Teachers in Secondary School.* Network Continuum.

Unser, B. in. Wright, M.P. (2003). *The Coaches' Chalkboard.* iUniverse.

Wilson, R. quoted in Wyche, S. (Jan. 29, 2014). Russell Wilson's fortitude lifted Seattle Seahawks to Super Bowl. Retrieved from: http://www.nfl.com/superbowl/story/0ap2000000319378/article/russell-wilsons-fortitude-lifted-seattle-seahawks-to-super-bowl

Winfrey, O. (n.d.) http://business.com

Photo Credits

About the Author: Georgi Dolence
Student-Athlete Profile: Paula Gambrell Maxwell

About the Author

My name is Robert Grilli, I'm 5'9 175lbs (as per my baseball roster), have the ability to grow a mean beard which I attribute to my country of origin as it serves as a blanket of warmth during the perceived 365 days of igloo weather and polar bear riding season. Jokes aside, I am from Canada, born and raised. I attended St. Dunstan Elementary school. I graduated from St. Michael's College school (SMC) in downtown Toronto at 17 and left home at 18. I attended Salt Lake Community College in Utah for two years, I was recruited to and graduated from the University of Houston with Bachelor of Science in Economics with a minor in Business in Spring 2016.

Student-Athlete Profile

Tale of the Tape
Vital Statistics

Name: Robert Grilli
Height: 5'9
Weight: 175 lbs
Beard: Full
Country of Origin: Canada

Education:
Elementary: St. Dunstan's
High School: St. Michael's College School
College: Salt Lake Community College
University: University of Houston

Made in the USA
Columbia, SC
30 August 2017